Graham Nicholson was Curator of York
Castle Museum from 1979 to 1985.
The Museum contains an extraordinary
collection of kitchen equipment, dating from the
seventeenth century to the present day.

In this book, the author combines his
interest in those kitchens of another
age with a practical knowledge of cookery.

English Cottage
COOKERY

Graham Nicholson

York Castle Museum

ISBN 0 900264 15 2

Published by
York Castle Museum
York YO1 1RY

Printed by
Hindson Print, Newcastle upon Tyne

Designed by
Steve Moore

Text
©Graham Nicholson 1985

Illustrations
©York Castle Museum 1985

Contents

Preface

I hope this is a practical book. The styles of cooking it describes belong to the eighteenth and nineteenth centuries, but there is nothing here that cannot be attempted with success in the modern kitchen.

The recipes contain my interpretations. Such instructions as "Turn two quarts of new milk to curd and press the whey from it . . ." are likely to be baffling. The quantities are too huge for a modern family, intended as they are for a household of master, wife, numerous children and servants. Moreover the methods (such as turning milk to curd by adding buttermilk to warm milk) are unfamiliar and not always successful with modern and refined ingredients. I trust, nonetheless, that I have not altered the spirit of these traditional dishes.

The cottager's means were limited and his table furnished with economy. At times of dearth many families eked out an existence on tea, white bread (bought from a baker), potatoes and a little bacon and dripping. In better times, and in months of plenty, the cottager and his family could produce much of their own needs. His pig, his hens, orchard, garden or 'potato ground', and possibly his cow, provided a substantial supplement to the flour and meat which were purchased at local markets. This was a wholesome and nutritious diet, but if your interest is in *cuisine minceur* you should put this book away immediately. Calories loom pretty large in some of the recipes.

It goes without saying that there are few exotic ingredients, though by the eighteenth century even the cottager's table reflected Britain's success as a colonizing power. Potatoes had come from America, rice was imported from India, sugar from the West Indies. Spices brought from the East Indies were expensive, but nutmeg, mace (the outer husk of nutmeg) and cinnamon were commonly available.

It follows that everything needed for cottage cookery is cheap and available. If you stick to the sound advice to eat foods in season, these recipes require no use of deep freeze or tin-opener.

Happy eating!

Introduction

Over the past hundred years or so our eating habits have been transformed and time-honoured ways of cooking have been largely forgotten.

Cottage cooking is to do with using the locally-grown foodstuffs to make satisfying and economical dishes. Because farming conditions varied considerably from county to county, there was a distinct regional variation in diet. While the southerner had wheaten bread, the northerner had oatcake cooked on a griddle. In 1797 Sir Frederic Eden observed that farmers in the north tended to boil meat, vegetables and puddings in an iron pot over the fire, which is a most ancient method of cooking, going back to pre-history. By contrast, southerners roasted meat before the fire and baked bread in an oven. This was culturally a more advanced mode of cooking, associated with the higher social classes.

One of the problems of assembling this book has been that ordinary people rarely wrote down their recipes. They prepared food as mother and grandmother had done before them. It was a kind of vernacular cookery which did not rely on written instructions.

So how do we know what ordinary people ate? There are the observations of travellers, such as the intrepid Celia Fiennes who recorded in 1698, in Kendal, that:

here it was I saw the oat Clap bread made . . . . they have no other sort of bread unless at market towns.

She gives a detailed account of the skilled process of making oat bread. Another way is to consider the kitchen equipment that our forebears used. In the fine collection at York Castle Museum there are grates, stoves, ovens, spits, pans and devices of one sort or another which give an insight into the way food has been cooked over several hundred years. I have included a short description of the cottager's kitchen later on.

There *is* a written tradition of English cooking, which culminates in Mrs Beeton's *Book of Household Management* in the latter part of the nineteenth century. A household in this sense means a place with a retinue of servants who could purchase, concoct and serve the elaborate fare thought proper for a wealthy family.

Mrs Beeton's predecessors were the wives of the country gentry who, in the seventeenth and eighteenth centuries, collected recipes for use in their own kitchens. One that I have used was Elizabeth Moxon whose *English Housewifery Exemplified* of 1741 is the earliest Yorkshire cook book. Another compilation which runs through dozens of editions in the eighteenth and nineteenth centuries is Mrs Rundell's *New System of Domestic Cookery.* Both these ladies were accomplished cooks and some of their recipes were beyond the means of a cottager, but they include much simpler recipes which use local produce economically. I take this to be a hallmark of cottage cookery.

One nineteenth century cookbook stands out. It is Alexis Soyer's *A Shilling Cookery for the People.* Soyer was the most celebrated chef of his day and the patron of fashionable restaurants. He was equally interested in the food of the poor and in the preface to his *Shilling Cookery* he wrote:

whilst semi-buried in my fashionable culinary sanctorum

of the Reform Club, surrounded by the elite of society . . .
. I could not gain . . . . the slightest knowledge of Cottage
life. Determined to carry out my long thought of project, I
cheerfully bade adieu to my wealthy employers . . . . and .
. . . I set forth on my journey, visiting on my route every
kind philanthropic and useful institution, but more
especially the domains of that industrial (i.e. industrious)
class, the backbone of every free country – the People.

Soyer travelled to the north, and particularly to Yorkshire.
He visited asylums, hospitals and mines. The general
ignorance of the poor in cooking disturbed him, and what
he offers is really a reformed cottage cookery, based on the
ingredients and kitchen equipment available to the
cottager, with methods better judged to preserve the
nutritional value of the food.

This little book cannot hope to be a history of the common
man's food. I hope it might contribute, however, in a
popular way to an understanding of the everyday life of our
forebears.

The Cottage Kitchen

Inside the English cottage domestic activity centred around the fire. This single source of heat afforded not only the warmth around which the family gathered, but also their light in the evening, their cooking, their hot water for washing and for laundry. It preserved the hams hung in the chimney, dried the clothes – in short it was the universal provider.

But the fireplace itself was to be transformed. At its simplest, the medieval cottager's hearth had been no more than a pile of small wood or turf, gathered laboriously from the common or moor. Smoky as it must have been, the fire was laid in the centre of the room or against a wall, under a

Illustration: The Albert Kitchener

smoke hood. Over the smouldering embers, a large iron-pot was suspended, in which all manner of boiling, stewing and seething was performed. Incredibly, in the so-called black houses of Orkney, this tradition was perpetuated into the early years of the twentieth century.

In Georgian and Victorian England, as canals and railways spread across the country, and mining technology improved, coal was more widely available. Coal burns best when raised from the floor; and this forced a break with the age-old tradition of wood and turf fires at hearth level. Moreover, for economy, coal needs to be restricted to a small basket. Stone hobs were installed in fireplaces and were joined by iron fire-bars to make a simple grate. The hobs were useful perches for pots and pans. Then, around 1800, stone hobs began to be replaced by cast-iron. When, a few years later, a door was added to one hob, and a lid to the other, a somewhat primitive oven and boiler was formed. The Victorian cast-iron range was born.

Both economy and convenience were served by the new arrangements, at least in theory. One good central fire could boil, roast, bake and provide comfort for the family. In early, pre-Victorian ranges there was often provision for separate fires under the oven and boiler, no doubt for warm days when a roaring blaze in the central grate was not welcome. The boiler was at first a more successful appliance than the oven, though both had their drawbacks. With the boiler, its small capacity and the slow, rather dangerous process of extracting hot water by ladle were the main problems. Rust and lime-scale were further hazards, though the latter could be avoided: rain water collected from the roof was preferred for shaving and for washing. After about 1840, a tap was normally fitted to the front of the boiler. The cast-iron ovens were heated by direct contact with the fire.

They were slow to warm up and then extremely hot on one side, which made for unsatisfactory cooking. A number of expedients were tried: an iron bar set across the fire and through the wall of the oven to conduct heat, or an oven set higher and to the rear of the firebox, the housewife being obliged to reach across the hot coals to attend to her cooking. Some ovens even contained a turntable arrangement, so that a cake could be turned regularly. The solution, only widely adopted in the second half of the century, was an arrangement of flues and dampers which directed hot air from the fire to all sides of the oven.

By general consent, the enclosed iron oven was not particularly good at roasting meat. Fat fell onto very hot surfaces and was burnt, tainting the flavour of the joint. Nothing could match spit-roasting, but few had the scale of fire equipment to do the job. Instead, the tinplate dutch oven was placed before the range: its polished interior reflected the heat of the fire onto meat hanging within. When the juices ran down into a dripping tray, the cottager opened a rear door and began to baste. The heat of the fire would soon char the meat, so it was steadily turned to and fro by a clockwork bottle-jack which hung from the top of the dutch oven. The cottager of more limited means could

Illustration: The Tinplate Dutch Oven

---

hang his meat on a twisted thread of wool, which had the same effect.

Toasters were natural adjuncts to the open fire. They came in a variety of ingenious forms and might stand on their own legs or be attached to the fire-bars. They were useful for bread, bacon, kippers and any small piece of food. Some even had rotating heads so that toast could be turned to a perfectly uniform colour. Cooking vessels could be supported in front of the fire on an iron trivet, or suspended above it on a chimney crane and pot-hook.

Scores, if not hundreds of iron-founders produced sets of fireplace 'fixtures', as the ovens and boilers were called. They were the first type of consumer durable sold to a mass market. But they were unconsidered in design. A local blacksmith would set the fixtures in the fireplace (still habitually a wide, arched opening), finishing the job by fitting the fire-bars which joined oven to boiler. The wide chimney and uncontrolled rush of air to the fire made for a prodigal use of fuel. One of the worst aspects was the amount of heat that radiated into the room – a welcome fault in winter, no doubt, but wearisome in summer when the fire was still needed for cooking and hot water.

In the second half of the century, manufacturers made some modest improvements. Fully enclosed ranges or kitcheners appeared around 1850. Their iron framework filled the whole chimney opening. The throat of the flue was restricted and the fire was enclosed beneath a continuous hotplate; some ranges had fire-doors which almost turned them into closed stoves. It was not all gain. Free to draw air through the ashpit, ranges burnt all too well. Whether cooking or not, and despite dampers, they quite frequently melted their wrought-iron fire-bars. A useful addition was the moveable plate or cheek which reduced the size of the firebox; it was wound into position by a rack and pinion device. By the end of the century, the range was a complex elaboration of the original idea. Hot plates, warming shelves, trivets, fire-bar extensions and stands, pot cranes, sometimes an additional oven and a hanging rail on the mantle-piece, for drying socks and stockings: all had been squeezed close to the precious fire.

Compare the kitchen of today. All the work-saving devices have their independent source of power. The electric kettle, toaster, grill and iron are ready for service at a moment's notice. In the cottage, a similar level of convenience was provided centrally by the ever-glowing range.

A peculiarity of some northern and upland kitchens should be mentioned. The backstone or bakestone was in essence no more than a flat piece of stone which could be heated, but many houses in the eighteenth and nineteenth centuries had a sizeable built-in stone table to one side of the fireplace. Its purpose was the production of oat-cakes, which were a staple in areas where wheat could not be grown. Oatmeal will not work into a dough, but mixed with water or milk, and left overnight, it forms a thin batter or soft paste. The batter when poured onto a hot bakestone solidifies quickly. It must be moved to a cooler part of the stone for the first part of the drying process. Finally it was hung in the kitchen, over a creel or wooden framework suspended from the ceiling. In smaller kitchens the place of the backstone was often taken by a circular iron griddle which could be hung over the fire.

The Iron Pot:
Stews, Soups and Broths

Alexis Soyer rightly judged the antiquity of the iron pot:

> . . . . Every cottage throughout the land has a peculiarity
> in cookery and cooking utensils which neither place nor
> time can erase . . . . In winter, when all nature is desolate,
> when heavy frost spreads his mantle over the myriads of
> defunct flowers, then this homely king rallies round him
> his subjects, to entertain, comfort, and feed them, and
> make them happy . . . . This is no other than the
> three-legged iron pot, who has done such good service for
> so many generations.

The long reign of the iron pot stretches back into the Middle Ages. It supplanted the pottery cooking vessel, which had fulfilled much the same purpose for hundreds of years. In the cottage the boiling pot had numerous advantages, economical, nutritional and technological. Firstly, any and every sort of meat can be boiled. Even the most unpromising, and least expensive parts of an animal – the feet, hocks, shanks and knuckles – will become tender and yield up their goodness in time. Secondly, a single pot often sufficed to cook *all* the family's food. Vegetables, dumplings, puddings, sometimes suspended in cloth nets, could be added and subtracted from the simmering liquid as necessary. The nutritional advantage of keeping the juices and fats of the meat in a liquid which was then used for broth may not have been as apparent to cottagers as it was to some cookery writers; but the thrifty cottager knew that a roast of meat shrank visibly in cooking. But until the later nineteenth century, when manufactured iron ranges were widely sold, most cottagers simply had no choice. They had no oven, nor could they have afforded the fuel to fire one, so it is correct to say that the iron pot over the open fire was the *most* important medium of cookery until our own century.

The distinctions between stews, soups and broths, pottage and porridge were not very marked, because each was really a part or stage of the others. We can follow the process of iron pot cooking from Esther Copley's *Complete Cottage Cookery* of about 1845.

A piece of meat was first boned, and then the bones and gristly parts simmered for several hours in a closed pot. (Mrs Copley suggests that during this stage a pudding in a cloth can be boiled.) This produces a stock in which the meat, with any herbs, seasonings and spices, can be cooked. About an hour before the meat is done, any and all manner of root vegetables, green vegetables, onions, parboiled potatoes and dumplings can be added. The result we recognize and enjoy as a stew. These processes need a large quantity of liquid. It was vital to the cottage economy as it forms a basis of one or more additional meals. The final process, therefore, was the thickening. For this a number of ingredients was available. Excavated medieval cooking pots have been found to contain all manner of grain, including varieties that we would regard as weed seeds. Real poverty and hunger were no doubt the cause. Traditionally, pearled (that is hulled) barley was used. It was sometimes soaked overnight before use, and then boiled with the stock for at least two hours to make a broth. Rice was freely available in the nineteenth century and could be used similarly, though it required much shorter cooking. Dried peas, either hulled and split or whole, or dried kidney beans were frequently used. An alternative was to add oatmeal, mixed first with a little liquid; such oat-based dishes were known as porridge, pottage or gruel and were important parts of the diet in northern England and Scotland.

Pot Luck

Here Alexis Soyer describes the iron pot classic. It is a two-stage recipe – first day the slowly cooked meat, the next the thickened broth. Nowadays your largest, heaviest saucepan or iron casserole must take the part of the three-legged pot.

**2 lb beef, either brisket, flank or skirt
4 pints cold water
1 lb peeled potatoes
1 lb other root vegetables in season
such as carrots, parsnips, turnips or fresh peas
salt and pepper
bay leaf**

Serves 6

Place the meat, water, bay leaf and a teaspoonful of salt in the pan and boil gently for 3 hours. The pan should be covered.

About 45 minutes before serving add the vegetables and a good pinch of pepper. Add more boiling water if necessary to cover the contents of the pan.

Before serving, set the meat on a warm dish and allow to cool for about 10–15 minutes. This rest will improve the texture of the meat, and make it easier to carve. Meanwhile, take about a pint of liquid from the pan for gravy, and if it needs thickening, reduce it by boiling briskly in a small saucepan.

Carve the meat, drain the vegetables (retaining the stock) and serve.

Broth

And now for stage two: the *broth*, which, by tradition, you make the following day. Add to the stock:

4 oz of split peas
8 oz of mixed vegetables
(e.g. carrots, white cabbage, turnips)
1 oz brown sugar

Boil slowly until the split peas and vegetables are cooked. With a few hunks of bread, it makes a nourishing meal in itself.

Boiled Ham

Almost every cottager with a little land kept a pig. It was his insurance against destitution. Either he could kill it as the winter approached, salting down as much as could be preserved, or he could sell it for cash. Boiling was preferred, because baking or roasting caused shrinkage.

So boiled ham took on the status of a special dish for high days, holidays and family gatherings, a status it retained among working people of Victorian and Edwardian cities. It was an essential of a proper high tea and many a man's wish was "to be buried with boiled 'am" – in other words, to have a respectable funeral.

Unfortunately the texture and taste of most commercially-available boiled ham is spoiled by its artificially high content of water and gelatinous matter. It bears no comparison with the real thing, which for preference should be cooked in a large piece on the bone. This is an old recipe of Mrs Isobelle Gott of Lothersdale, collected by Joan Poulson in her Yorkshire Cookery.

5 lb ham on the bone
8 cloves
6 peppercorns
3 bay leaves
1 clove garlic
breadcrumbs

Serves at least 12

Soak the ham overnight in cold water. Put into fresh water and boil for 5 minutes. Drain and again put the ham in clean water, adding the cloves, peppercorns, bay leaves and garlic. Cover and cook slowly for 3 hours or until tender. Leave to cool in the liquor, then skin and rub the fat over with browned breadcrumbs. Slice thinly to serve.

Boiled Leg of Mutton

Mutton was once a regular ingredient of English cooking, but with the arrival of frozen young lamb from New Zealand, available all year round, it has fallen out of fashion. Mutton is rarely offered by the butcher, so you will have to order it in advance. The very best mutton are the wethers, the male sheep raised especially for mutton, but these are hard to come by, most being sought by restaurants and hotels. You will probably be offered a ewe. Remember the joints of mutton are much larger than joints of lamb – a leg may weigh anything from 5 lb upwards.

1 leg of mutton
1 onion
1 carrot
1 stick of celery
sprig of rosemary or sage
1 clove
6 juniper berries
1 pig or calf's foot, or bacon rind
salt
pepper

Trim any excess fat from the mutton. Cut the shank bone through, but include it in the pot.

Take a large pot or saucepan and put the joint in with enough boiling water to cover, and 1 teaspoon of salt per pound of meat. Add the other ingredients; the onion and carrot should be roughly chopped. Bring to the boil and reduce to a simmer. Skim off any scum. Cover and keep at the simmer for 25 minutes per pound of meat, with 25 minutes over. Drain, allow to cool a little before carving and serving.

Strain the liquid for use as the basis for broth.

Pea Soup

Peas of various forms have been an important food for ordinary people from medieval times. They were dried for storage, and the old varieties had a high starch content – like the marrowfat or 'mushy' peas available today. Pease pudding was a nourishing if slightly dull affair. Traditional pea soup, however, needs no apology in any surroundings.

**3 pints ham stock
12 oz dried peas
teaspoon mustard powder
2 onions
salt
pepper**

Serves 4

The ideal stock is the liquor in which boiled ham has been cooked. If that is not available a friendly butcher should be able to provide some ham bones to boil for 3 hours. Or you can add 6 oz chopped lean bacon to the soup, at the simmering stage.

Place the peas in boiling water and soak overnight. Strain and place the peas and other ingredients in a large pan. Cover and simmer gently for 3 hours, adding more water if necessary.

Oxtail Soup

This is a cross between a soup and a stew. Oxtail is uniquely rich in flavour and the gelatinous content of the bones is high. The result is a strong and thick soup or sauce served with the oxtail; the lucky eater scrapes or even sucks the meat from the bone.

**1 oxtail
1 onion
1 large carrot
1 large turnip
4 sticks of celery
3 oz butter
2 oz flour
salt
pepper
4 cloves**

Serves 4

Cut up the oxtail and steep in boiling water for 15 minutes. Remove and dry the meat. Keep the water. Prepare and chop the vegetables into small pieces.

In an iron casserole melt half the butter and fry the meat and vegetables for a few minutes. Add the water, cloves and seasonings, cover and simmer for 4 hours. Skim off any froth from the surface of the stock.

Melt the remaining butter in a saucepan, and stir in the flour to make a roux. Cook for 2–3 minutes. Strain off the stock, and add it little by little to the roux. Stir well.

Pour this sauce back over the oxtail and serve.

Traditional Oatmeal Porridge

We owe our familiar flattened porridge oats to that Victorian invention, the roller mill. Before that, porridge was made from oatmeal and, personally, I prefer its nuttier flavour and texture.

The main ingredient of success with porridge is long cooking. Forget the 'one minute' idea – even if you are using modern porridge oats. Always opt for porridge if you are staying in a large hotel. The pot has been on the hob since 7.00 a.m., and by the time you emerge at a civilised hour, the porridge will be excellent. Porridge is associated with Scotland, but it was equally a dish of Lancashire and the North-West, where it could cook for long hours in the three-legged iron pot.

**½ cup of oatmeal
1 pint of water
a little salt**

To serve:
milk or cream, sugar or butter.

Serves 2

Start with boiling water in a medium-sized saucepan. Add the oatmeal little by little, stirring briskly all the time. Bring back to the boil, still stirring; cover the pan and simmer for 15 minutes. Now add the salt, stir and cover again to cook for a least 15 minutes, preferably more.

Serve with milk or cream. Traditionally porridge is eaten as a savoury, without sugar. I like it with sugar, but, as an alternative, try adding a knob of butter when you serve.

Open-fire Cooking

Great houses possessed elaborate equipment for roasting meat – spits, clockwork mechanisms, dripping pans, special basting spoons. The cottager had none of these. By the late nineteenth century he may have had a tin-plate roasting screen within which he could hang his joint. Soyer did not really approve of roasting in the cottage, because it was not economical; better, roasting cuts of meat were not necessarily more nutritious than the cheapest pieces, and in the process of cooking much weight was lost. Nonetheless, he described a 'simple plan of roasting before the fire'. It is a perfectly practical method that can be used at home, provided that you have either an old-fashioned mantle-piece with an overhanging shelf, such as every cottage had, or can put a hook firmly into a ceiling some 9 to 12 inches in front of an open fireplace. The equipment you require is a joiner's G cramp, to clamp to the mantlepiece, two steel S hooks, some strong woollen thread, a dripping pan, a stick forked at one end and, of course an open fire. Soyer clearly intended his method for use before a coal fire.

Here is Soyer's method:

> In the first place, the fire must be made up, and cleared from ashes. Place before it the dripping-pan, and from above the fire, suspend from a hook a piece of worsted thread, sufficiently strong to bear the joint, and a hook suspended at the end. Have a piece of stick forked at one end, which place against the mantle piece, so that it keeps the thread at a sufficient distance from the fire. By having two pieces of stick, the distances can be easily managed. Twist the worsted; put on the joint; give it a sufficient distance from the fire. This is quite equal to either a smoke or bottle-jack for cottage use.

The twisted thread, sometimes called a dangle-spit, was an age-old device to keep the meat turning before the fire.

Timings:

With open-fire roasting it is important to begin with the meat close to a hot fire, say 12 inches, for the first 10 minutes. This helps to seal in the juices. Thereafter move the meat away, to about 18 inches, and the fire may be allowed to decline a little. This method of roasting is best with a substantial piece of meat, say a minimum of 3 lbs. Unless the meat is very fat, it should be basted from time to time with the dripping. Exact cooking times cannot be given; too much depends on the heat of the fire, but you can expect the cooking to be quicker than for meat baked in an oven.

Roast Chicken

Again this is Soyer's way:

Hang it [the chicken] up with worsted, about ten inches from the fire, let it hang for ten minutes to set the skin, then press into a wooden spoon a piece of butter or hard dripping; when the skin is very hot rub it over with the fat in the spoon until all is melted, then draw it back to about twelve inches: a good sized fowl will take three quarters of an hour. Do not baste, but dredge with flour, after having rubbed it over with butter.

Gravy

I am frequently surprised that quite capable cooks seem unable to make gravy without recourse to cubes of this or packets of that, which usually contain monosodium glutumate and excessive salt. So here's a good, traditional, thick gravy which perfectly complements roasted or baked meat and poultry:

plain flour
½ pint of stock or water
salt and pepper to taste

Take the roasting pan into which the juices and fat of the meat have dripped. Set the meat aside in a warm place. (This few minutes rest will make it easier to carve.) Pour away some of the fat. Mix into the remaining fat and juices one or more tablespoons of flour, enough to form a roux or runny paste. Place the pan on the stove at a quick heat and cook the roux for 2 minutes. (This is important: it bursts the gluten in the flour and improves its texture and taste.) Heat the stock or water and add it little by little to the roux, mixing well with a wooden spoon. Bring to boil. Taste, and adjust the seasoning. Strain through a coarse sieve and serve.

Savoury Puddings and Pies

It is a commonplace that a pudding, served at the beginning of the meal, filled the belly and saved the meat. The saying in Yorkshire was "Them as eats most pudding 'as moast meat". But it would be quite wrong to regard puddings as dull stodge. They are one of the great strengths of English cooking, and surprisingly varied.

First there are the batter puddings. Yorkshire pudding is the most famous. But there are also paste puddings (including the immortal suet dumpling) and bread puddings, though the latter are often sweet. They can be boiled or baked, plain or fancy. All are economical, simple and nourishing.

Yorkshire Pudding

Yorkshire pudding is cooked in the hot fat from roasting beef. In a large kitchen with a spit, the dripping was caught in a tray beneath the meat, and the pudding cooked there; the cottager baked his in the dripping pan within his tin-plate roasting screen. The pudding emerged round and crisp at the edges, it was moist but light in the centre, with all the marvellous flavour of the meat juices.

4 oz plain flour
2 eggs
⅓ pint milk and water
salt and pepper
3 tablespoons of beef dripping

Serves 4

Sift the flour into a basin and make a well in the centre. Break the eggs into it and beat them into the flour, adding the milk and water little by little. Add the salt and pepper and beat the mixture until it is smooth.

Put the dripping in a baking tin (about 9×9 inches) and heat in the oven at 450°F/gas mark 8 for about 10 minutes. The dripping should be sizzling when you pour in the batter. Place it immediately on an upper shelf of the oven. Cook for about 25–30 minutes and serve immediately; a Yorkshire pudding kept waiting soon goes limp.

Season or Savoury Pudding

A bread pudding which can be served as an alternative to Yorkshire pudding.

1 lb white bread
4 oz suet
2 eggs
8 oz of boiled and chopped onions
sage
marjoram
nutmeg
salt and pepper
cup of milk

Serves 6

Break the bread into a mixing bowl and pour on sufficient milk (or water) to moisten it. Mash with a fork, and mix in the onion, suet, beaten eggs, herbs and spices. Grease a baking tin well. Spread the mixture evenly in the tin and bake for 30 minutes at 400°F/gas mark 6, until it is crisp and golden.

Toad in the Hole

This dish has survived to the present day, but is now generally a rather dull concoction of sausages in batter. The Victorian toad was more varied in its countenance. Soyer gives nearly a dozen different forms, including a recipe for six larks, each skewered and wrapped in bacon. This is less exotic and a good way of using up leftovers.

For the batter:
3 oz flour
2 eggs
½ pint milk
salt and pepper
a little nutmeg

For the contents:
1 lb cold roast meat, such as beef, pork or lamb
2 medium sized potatoes
2 medium sized onions

Serves 4

To prepare the batter, mix the eggs into the flour, and then beat in enough milk to achieve a runny consistency. Season with salt, pepper and grated nutmeg. Set on one side.

Cut the meat into pieces about the size of a small egg. Slice the onions and potatoes and arrange them with the meat in a well-greased baking dish. Season with salt and pepper. Pour in the batter. Bake for about 1 hour at about 375°F/gas mark 5.

Meat Pudding

The image of meat puddings has been sadly tarnished by the glutinous, manufactured efforts served up by unimaginative innkeepers. But the meat pudding has an honourable history. By slow cooking, inexpensive materials are transformed into delicious and nourishing fare for a cold day. It is a form of paste pudding.

For the paste:
9 oz flour
3 oz suet
salt
water to mix

For the filling:
1 lb stewing steak, such as flank or skirt
salt
pepper
¼ pint gravy or rich stock or brown ale

Serves 4

Rub half the suet into the flour with a pinch of salt. Moisten with water – just enough to hold the mixture together. Roll out on a floured board and spread the remainder of the suet over the paste. Fold it over, and beat with the rolling pin. Then roll it out, not too thinly. (The paste can be made several hours beforehand and rolled out just before use.)

Take a heat-proof basin, in which you will cook the pudding, and use it to mark out the circle of paste that you will need later for the upper crust. Set the circle of paste on one side.

Grease the basin well. If you want to be really traditional, you should spread a pudding cloth in the basin, but this is not essential. Line the basin with paste.

The meat should be cut into small pieces – about ½″ cubes. Arrange it in the basin and add salt, pepper and the stock, gravy or brown ale. Press the upper crust to the lower crust. If you have a pudding cloth, tie it up over the pudding. Cover well – baking foil is ideal, if not exactly authentic.

Place in a large, covered saucepan of boiling water for at least 3 hours, preferably 4. Do not allow the water to boil over the top of the basin; add extra boiling water as necessary.

Baked Meat Pudding

This is a batter pudding and it requires better cuts of meat than can be used in a boiled pudding. It is a good way of extending a small amount of meat to make a filling supper.

1 lb beefsteak
salt
pepper

For the batter:
3 eggs
2 tablespoons suet
1 lb flour
½ pint milk

Serves 4

Cut the meat into ½″ cubes and place in a greased oven-proof dish. Add salt and pepper to taste.

Make the batter by rubbing the suet into the flour. Then mix in the eggs, and finally add the milk a little at a time, beating hard with a whisk to achieve a smooth consistency. Pour the batter over the meat and cook for 1½ hours at 425°F/gas mark 7. Reduce the heat to 375°F/gas mark 5 after half an hour.

West Riding Pancake

A very simple and quick form of batter pudding.

2 oz of flour
½ cup milk
1 egg
salt and pepper
4 slices streaky bacon

Serves 1 or 2

Make up the batter by mixing the egg into the flour in a bowl, and then adding milk little by little until a runny consistency is achieved. Add salt and pepper, and set to one side.

Fry the bacon in a heavy pan. Remove the bacon from the pan, leaving the hot fat.

Pour the batter into the pan, and cook until the pancake is light brown, first on one side, then on the other. Lay on the slices of bacon, fold the pancake over, and serve immediately.

Lancashire Hot-pot

The hot-pot was a very popular dish in the textile towns of the north. It could be left all day on the hob or oven of the range to provide an inexpensive and satisfying meal when the family returned from the mill. Traditionally it was made with mutton, but cuts of lamb or beef can also be used. Pickled red cabbage is the time-honoured accompaniment, its sharp tang contrasting well with the rich aroma of the meat.

**4 mutton chops, or
1 lb lamb or beef stewing steak
1 lb onions
1½ lb potatoes
6 medium carrots
flour
bay leaf
1 teaspoon sugar
salt
pepper
dripping or lard for frying**

Serves 4

Pre-heat the oven to 350°F/gas mark 4 and heat within it a large earthenware or iron casserole. It should have a lid.

Put a little flour, with salt and pepper, on a plate. Dip the meat in it, to cover all surfaces, and then brown in hot dripping or fat in a frying pan.

Chop the onion into rings. Peel and slice the potatoes and carrots.

Now arrange the meat, onions, carrots and potatoes in layers in the casserole, ending with potatoes and a sprinkling of flour on top.

Add a tablespoon of flour to the frying pan and mix in with the fat. Add a bay leaf and about ¼ pint of boiling water; enough to make a thin gravy. Cook this, stirring well for 3 minutes, adding more water as necessary. Pour it over the contents of the casserole, cover and cook in the oven for 2 hours.

Remove the lid and cook for a further 10 minutes to brown the potatoes.

Pickled Red Cabbage

1 medium sized red cabbage
2 pints malt vinegar
salt
2 teaspoons allspice
2 teaspoons peppercorns

Remove the outer leaves and stalk of the cabbage and then slice it finely into strips. Place in a large bowl, sprinkle with salt and leave overnight.

Boil the vinegar with the allspice and peppercorns for an hour. Pour the vinegar, through a sieve to remove the spice and pepper, over the cabbage. Cover and leave overnight.

Drain the cabbage, place in jars and cover with cold vinegar. Seal the jars with greaseproof paper tied around the neck, and store in a cool place.

Shepherds Pie

Cottage cookery must have relied heavily on ways of re-using cooked fragments of meat. The main rule in such dishes is to give the meat a long second cooking, as cooked meat first becomes very tough on reheating.

**12 oz chopped cooked lamb or mutton
1 large onion
1 oz (bacon) dripping
1 lb mashed potatoes
½ pint stock or gravy
2 oz butter**

Serves 4

Remove any skin or gristle and any larger pieces of fat from the meat, but leave some fat. Chop the meat into small pieces, or mince if you prefer.

Chop and fry the onion in the dripping. Add this to the meat in an ovenproof dish; stir in the seasoning and gravy or stock.

Mix the butter into the mashed potato (which should be really well mashed into a puree). Spread the mash on top of the meat. Bake for 30–40 minutes at 400°F/gas mark 6.

If you wish, the top can be browned further by grilling.

Cottage Pork Pie

This is a variant of shepherd's pie, which uses the products of the cottage garden – apples, potatoes and pork.

12 oz chopped cooked pork
1 large onion
1 large or 2 small apples
1 lb mashed potatoes
salt
pepper
a leaf of sage
½ pint stock or gravy
2 oz butter

Serves 3 to 4

Proceed in the same manner as for shepherd's pie (see previous page). The apples should be peeled, cored and ringed, and placed under the potato top.

Potato Cakes

Potatoes became a popular crop, especially in the north, in the eighteenth century. They grew well on indifferent land, and were ideally suited to the cottager's garden.

Potato cakes, sometimes known as potato bread, can be served savoury or sweet.

1 lb potatoes
2 oz butter
4 oz flour
top of a pint of milk
grated nutmeg
pepper
salt

Serves 4

Peel, boil and mash the potatoes. Stir in the butter, milk, salt, pepper and nutmeg. Mix in sufficient flour to make a dough.

Roll out to between ¼" and ½" thickness, cut into 2" rounds, and cook on a hot, greased griddle or frying pan until each side is browned. Alternatively, cook on a greased tray in the oven for about 20 minutes. Serve hot and buttered.

To make sweet potato cakes, cut the dough thicker, say ¾", and when cooked, slice, spread with butter and brown sugar, and close. Serve on a hot dish.

Sweet Puddings

I have always been a great fan of real English puddings, and I suspect that there are countless others who share my enthusiasm. But where can one find these traditional creations today? They have been quietly dropped from the menus of hotels and restaurants, which seem to labour under the misapprehension that soggy gateaux and bought-in cremes caramels are the height of sophistication.

The last strongholds of the English pud are in those often reviled canteens which serve schools and work-places. Though they may mangle the fish and drown the vegetables, they have an unerring touch with the Spotted Dick, sponge puddings and Apple Charlotte. I suspect that this sacred tradition has been handed down through the conservative teaching of domestic science colleges. Long may it flourish!

Bread and Butter Pudding

It is a source of amazement that from such humble ingredients so splendid and delicious a pudding can be made. On top it is nutty brown, within (if all goes well) it rises to a sponge-like lightness.

6 slices of bread from a large white loaf
2 oz softened butter
3 oz of seedless raisins
3 average size eggs
2 oz caster sugar
1 pint milk
grated nutmeg

Serves 4

Butter a 2-pint pie dish. Butter each slice of bread and discard the crusts. Layer the bread in the dish, sprinkling raisins between the layers. Beat the eggs and sugar together. Heat the milk and add by degrees to the eggs and sugar; mix well and pour over the bread. Leave for 30 minutes.

Prepare a moderate oven, 350°F/gas mark 4. Sprinkle the pudding with nutmeg and bake for about 35 minutes until it is golden brown.

As Soyer says, the pudding may be done twenty different ways, by adding lemon-peel, orange-peel, cinnamon, mixed spices or fruit.

Pancakes

Shrove Tuesday, before the solemnity of Ash Wednesday and the Lenten period, was treated as a day of merriment. In the middle of the last century it was common for children to go Shroving. They went from house to house singing for money or food:

> *I come Shroving, a Shroving, a Shroving,*
> *For a piece of pancake,*
> *For a piece of truffle cheese,*
> *Of your own making,*

If the householder failed to comply, stones or pot sherds were thrown at his door.

8 oz flour
3 eggs
1 pint milk
salt
cinnamon or ginger

Makes about 9

Break the eggs into a basin and beat well. Sift the flour into another basin, and form a well in the centre. Add the eggs to the well and work in the flour well. Add the milk by degrees until it forms a batter. Add the ginger or cinnamon and salt.

Many people say that you should leave the batter for 2 or 3 hours in a cool place before using, but I have never found it made the slightest difference. Heat a frying pan with a teaspoon of lard or dripping. Pour off any excess fat, and then pour in just enough pancake batter to cover the floor of the pan. When the batter has set, loosen the edges with a spatula and turn it (or toss it if you are brave). When both sides of the pancake are a golden brown, dish up and serve with lemon and sugar.

It is perfectly possible to make pancakes in advance and to reheat in a warm oven.

Fritters

Fritters are small pancakes, enriched by any kind of fruit. Dried currants and apples seem to have been the favourites, but soft fruits such as raspberries and gooseberries can also be used. Fritters used to be eaten on Ash Wednesday – perhaps to use the batter remaining from Shrove Tuesday pancakes.

pancake mixture
4 medium baking apples, cored and chopped
6 oz currants
lard or dripping for frying

Serves 4

Mix the fruit into the batter, and drop tablespoons of the mixture into the very hot lard or dripping in a frying pan. In a large pan several can be prepared at once.

Turn once and cook till both sides are a pale golden brown. Drain, sprinkle with castor sugar and serve.

Spotted Dick

This is a hearty sort of pudding for a cold day, and, it must be said, it is no featherweight. I suppose you could lighten it with self-raising flour, but then it would lose its cottage origins.

12 oz plain flour
4 oz lb beef suet
4 oz currants
2 oz sugar
a little cinnamon
2 eggs
a cup of milk

Serves 6

Mix the flour, suet, currants, sugar and cinnamon together; beat the eggs lightly and mix in. Stir in the milk little by little, until a dough is formed. Place either in a heat-proof basin or a pudding cloth and boil in water for at least an hour and a half. Serve with custard or cream.

Plum Pudding

When Little Jack Horner put in his thumb, the plum he pulled out was not the Victoria or greengage, common residents of the cottage garden though they were. It was a Malaga raisin or a currant. Not every plum pudding was for Christmas, and this is a plainer version for everyday use.

8 oz plain flour
4 oz beef suet
4 oz currants
4 oz raisins or sultanas
pinch of allspice or cinnamon
2 oz soft brown sugar
1 egg
grated rind of a lemon
¼ pint of milk

Serves 6

Put all the dry ingredients in a mixing basin, make a well in the centre and mix in the eggs. Add the milk little by little until you achieve a rather sticky dough.

Turn the mixture into a buttered pudding bowl and cover tightly, or into a pudding cloth, and boil gently for about 3 hours.

Serve with custard or a sweet white sauce. The pudding can be reheated for another day by boiling for an hour.

Plum Pudding for Christmas

This is an easy to make Victorian pudding, and not too rich. It eschews brandy, rum and other spirits, which were beyond the cottager's purse. I don't think you will miss them, but you could always lace the white sauce with which this pudding is served.

8 oz raisins
8 oz currants
3 oz flour
3 oz white breadcrumbs, grated from a stale loaf
8 oz beef suet
6 oz brown sugar
2 oz mixed candied peel, finely chopped
¼ nutmeg, grated
4 eggs
water to mix

Serves 6 to 8

Mix all the dry ingredients thoroughly in a large mixing bowl. In a separate bowl, beat the eggs lightly and add to them half a cup of water. Now stir this very thoroughly indeed into the mixture. Add more water if necessary until it is well bound together but not so sticky that you cannot remove it cleanly from the bowl in one piece.

Butter 2 or 3 pudding basins (depending on their size) and fill to the brim with the mixture. Cover each pudding carefully with greaseproof paper and a pudding cloth (or foil) and tie tightly.

Steam for 4 hours. These puddings probably gain by being stored in a cool place for a week or more, so before use, steam them for a further 2 hours.

Mincemeat

This is a recipe from Mrs Hewlett's Complete Cook's Guide *of 1827.*

Mincemeat is a medieval idea. Originally it combined minced beef with the sweetness of fruit and spices. Nowadays, and by Mrs Hewlett's day, it was usual to omit the meat, but the beef suet remains to bind the mixture together. This is highly superior to the over-sweet purchased variety.

**1½ lb eating apples, pared, cored
and finely chopped
12 oz beef suet
12 oz seedless raisins
12 oz sugar
1 lemon, rind and juice
mace, cinnamon, cloves, (a pinch of each)
a little salt**

Optional:
**½ wineglass port and ½ wineglass of brandy
(or a wineglass of sweet white wine)**

Mix all the ingredients well together and press firmly in a deep pan. Store in a cool dry place and cook in pies and puddings.

Bread Pudding
for the Christmas Season

This is another of Mrs Hewlett's recipes, this time from her Complete Cottage Cookery, *and uses the mincemeat of her earlier recipe. It makes an interesting contrast to the usual boiled Christmas pudding.*

6 slices stale bread from a large white loaf
6 oz mincemeat
1 pint milk
2 standard eggs

Serves 4

Prepare a moderate oven, 350°F/gas mark 4. Butter a 2 pint pie dish. Remove the crusts from the bread and put a layer in the bottom of the dish. Spread it with a layer of mincemeat; then more bread and mincemeat until the dish is full. Finish with a layer of bread.

Beat the eggs and stir into them the milk, which should be hot but not boiling. Pour this over the pudding and bake for about 35 minutes until golden brown.

Rice Pudding

This is a delicious variation on the familiar rice pud'. Georgians and Victorians almost invariably added eggs to the mixture, and this helps to set the pudding in a custard-like consistency. Sometimes they added cream, currants or nutmeg, but the simple version is so good that it needs no elaboration. The traditional way is to boil first, and bake afterwards; it has the advantage that a fine pudding can be made in under an hour.

2 oz rice (short grain)
1 pint milk
2 oz butter
1 egg
1 oz sugar (or more if you have a sweet tooth)
lemon peel

Serves 4

Wash the rice in a sieve and place with the milk in a heavy saucepan or steampan. (Choose a large pan, as the pudding has a habit of boiling over.) Add the butter, sugar and lemon peel and bring it to the boil. Cover and simmer for about 20 minutes, or until the rice is tender. Remove from the heat.

Beat the egg well (both yolk and white) and mix quickly and thoroughly with the rest of the pudding. Pour into a deep pie dish and bake in a moderate oven, 300–350°F/gas mark 2–4, for about 30 minutes, or until it sets.

Sago Pudding

The star of my Yorkshire grandmother's somewhat limited culinary repertoire was sago pudding, cooked slowly in the oven of her coal-fired range. Sago is a starch produced in the trunk of the sago-palm, particularly in Borneo. It is rubbed through sieves into grains; the smaller type were known as pearl sago, the larger as bullet sago. By 1884, over 17,000 tons a year was being imported into Britain, enough by my reckoning to make 310 million sago puddings a year. This was clearly a very popular dish.

**2 oz sago
1 pint milk
1 oz sugar
lemon peel
cinnamon
nutmeg
1 egg**

Serves 4

The method is the same as that for rice pudding, the cinnamon and nutmeg being added to the milk at the outset.

Custard

There's not much wrong with the Bird's variety, but the real thing adds distinction to a pudding, or can be eaten just on its own.

1 pint milk
2 oz sugar
4 eggs
peel of half a lemon, thinly cut

Serves 4

Boil the milk and remove from the heat. Mix in the sugar and add the lemon peel. Break the eggs in a bowl and beat well with a fork. Little by little add the milk (which by this time should have cooled a little, and certainly should not be boiling). Mix well and pass through a sieve into a basin.

Stand the basin in a large saucepan containing an inch of hot water and heat very gently without stirring until the custard has thickened, which may take 20–30 minutes. And if it doesn't thicken, you will have to cheat by mixing thoroughly a level teaspoon of cornflour with a little warm milk, and adding the custard to it little by little, stirring well. Return the custard to its basin and to its hot water bath.

If the custard has curdled, however, there's not much you can do about it; try removing from the heat, adding cornflour, and beating very hard. If that fails, start again.

Potting and Jugging

Seasonal glut and seasonal dearth spurred the cottager to preserve food from one season to another. It is not, perhaps, a practical proposition in a modern kitchen to have a ham or a flitch of bacon hanging from the beams. But there are a number of old techniques that could be tried. They may not preserve food for more than a week or two, but they produce some interesting textures and spicy flavours.

Potted Beef

This version of a popular dish is based on a 1694 recipe of Mrs Ann Blencowe. Many early recipes are quite highly spiced, and this is no exception. It calls for the use of a mortar and pestle to make a paste – another characteristic of early cookery. You can leave out some of the flavourings if you prefer, and use a blender to save time and effort. Potted beef is excellent on sliced bread or hot toast.

1 lb stewing steak
3 oz butter
1 tablespoon salt
2 leaves of sage, well chopped
1 teaspoon chopped thyme
a little mace
grated nutmeg
pepper

Serves 6 to 8

Put the meat in a heavy pan with a little water and cook gently on the stove for an hour. Remove the meat from the pan and allow it to cool. Pare off all fat and skin, cut the meat finely, and add half the butter and the rest of the ingredients. Pound it into a smooth paste (or use the blender). Pack firmly into an earthenware pot or jar. Cover and stand it in a pan of boiling water for an hour. Allow to cool.

Melt the rest of the butter and pour over the meat in its pot. The butter should form a seal. Store in a cool place.

Whitby Polony

This is another form of potted meat, which can either be served in slices or spread on toast and sandwiches.

**1 lb lean beef
8 oz lb lean ham
8 oz white breadcrumbs
mace
nutmeg
pepper
salt**

Serves 6 to 8

Put the beef and ham through a mincing machine (or a blender). Mix in the breadcrumbs which should be finely crumbled. Season with a little mace, nutmeg, pepper and salt. Mix well.

Pack the mixture into an earthen or glass bowl, and seal well with two layers of greaseproof paper, tied securely.

Place the bowl and mixture into a saucepan of boiling water, cover and steam for 3½ hours. When it is cold, turn it out carefully on to a plate.

Haslet

An ancient dish, associated with the eastern part of England, and one that makes economical use of the liver and any other oddments of fresh pork.

8 oz pig's liver
1 lb pork
12 oz fine breadcrumbs
2 teaspoons chopped parsley and thyme
salt
pepper
½ cup of milk

Serve 4 to 6

Mince the pork and liver, and mix together with the breadcrumbs and other dry ingredients. Add just sufficient milk to bind the mixture together.

Grease a square meat tin (about 9″ square) and press in the mixture. Bake in a moderate oven, 375°F/gas mark 5, for 1½ hours. Cut into 3″ squares and serve hot or cold.

Potted Shrimps or Prawns

**8 oz shrimps or prawns
4 oz butter
salt and pepper
nutmeg
powdered cloves**

Serves 4

Shell the shrimps or prawns and season them with salt, white pepper and a very small amount of grated nutmeg and cloves. Pack them firmly into a pot on individual serving dishes. Add a piece of butter to each pot and bake in the oven for 15 minutes at 350°F/gas mark 4.

Remove from the oven and allow to cool. Seal each pot with hot butter and serve cold with brown bread.

Jugged Hare

The point of cooking a hare, or other game, in a jug is that little liquid is needed to cover the meat. The rich gravy of the dish will keep the hare succulent and tasty during long slow cooking in the oven. A good substitute, however, is a 'Nottingham jar' – an earthenware casserole with a well-fitting lid.

**1 hare
2 onions
2 carrots
1 stick celery
herbs to taste
1½ pints stock or water
1 tablespoon butter or dripping
juice of one lemon, and a little grated rind**

Serves 4

Joint the hare, wipe the pieces, and retain the blood. Fry the pieces to a good brown, and place in the jug with the sliced vegetables. Add the stock or water and lemon.

Cook about 3–4 hours in a slow oven, 300°F/gas mark 2, until the meat is tender. Strain the liquid into a saucepan. Add the wine and blood. Re-heat, but do not boil. Return the liquor to the jug. Cook for a further 15 minutes in the oven, and serve.

Breads, Cakes and Biscuits

It may be surprising to learn that there is no great tradition of bread baking in the English cottage. To be more precise, few cottagers had a suitable oven, or could afford the fuel to bake wheaten loaves. This can be readily understood when we read how bread was baked. These are Mrs Rundell's instructions:

> Put the fire into the oven; and by the time it is warm enough, the dough will be ready. Make the loaves about five pounds each: sweep out the oven very clean and quick, and put in the bread; shut it up close, and two hours and a half will bake it. . . . . The oven should be

round, not long; the roof from twenty to twenty-four inches high, the mouth small, and the door of iron, to shut close.

The essential point is that the fire (of faggots) was put *inside* a large brick oven; the bread then cooked by residual heat – very hot at first, then cooler, which is just as it should be. Incidentally, this gives the origins of the phrase 'the upper crust' as a name for people of rank. The 'very clean and quick' sweeping would not remove all the ash, embers and soot from the floor of the oven, and so the lower crust would be less palatable than the upper crust. You can guess which part of the bread went to the serving men and which was reserved to the master and mistress' table.

Such a method of baking was appropriate to a grand house. Other people bought their bread from the baker in town, and, incidentally, the preference for white bread is an English peculiarity, going back to medieval times. There is, nonetheless, a tradition of cottage bread-making, as opposed to bread-baking, especially in the north of England. It used the local staple, oats, more than wheat; for the most part, it did not use yeast or an oven. The typical cottage product was an oatcake, cooked on a flat backstone or griddle.

Oatcake

There are a variety of names – oatcake, havercake, deriving from the old Norse word 'hafre' meaning oats, and clapbread, that is beaten with the hand into thin cakes. There are two basic types – those made from batter, and those made from dough. Let's start with the batter variety. It forms a soft cake which can be eaten hot with butter. Traditionally it was packed away with a piece of cheese to become a ploughman's lunch. Or try toasting it with grated cheese mixed with beaten egg to form a rarebit.

**8 oz finely ground oatmeal
or 5 oz oatmeal and 3 oz plain flour
1 teaspoon bicarbonate of soda
1 pint milk and water
½ teaspoon salt**

Makes about 8 cakes

Unless the oatmeal is as finely ground as flour, use a mixture of oatmeal and plain flour. Mix the oatmeal, bicarbonate of soda and salt together, and add the milk and water to form a thin batter. Heat the lightly greased griddle, if you have one, or a solid frying pan. Pour a little of the mixture onto the griddle and spread it with a spatula. After about 2 or 3 minutes, when the edges begin to dry, slide a palette knife under the cake and turn it. Cook as long again, and then place the cake on a clean cloth to cool.

Muffins

Muffins are the wheaten equivalents of oatcakes, traditionally baked on a bakestone or griddle. The name seems to have come from the old French 'moufflet' meaning soft bread. They are eaten toasted and buttered for breakfast or tea.

1 lb flour
2 teaspoons sugar
⅓ pint tepid water
⅓ pint tepid milk
1 teaspoon salt
½ oz yeast

Makes about 12 muffins

Mix the yeast with a little of the milk and water into a smooth paste, gradually adding the remainder of the liquid, then the salt and sugar. Stir well.

Place the flour in a bowl, make a well in the centre and pour in the liquid. Work the flour in to make a soft dough.

Cover the bowl and leave it in a warm place for an hour, for the dough to rise. Knead the dough thoroughly and then divide into small flat rounds. Place them on a pastry board or work surface and cover with a warm cloth for 20 minutes until the muffins have risen.

To cook, place the muffins on a hot griddle, or thick frying pan, and cook for 10 minutes on each side, or until very slightly brown.

Fat Rascals

Another name for fat rascals is Turf Cakes, and they were cooked on a griddle or a yetling (a large closed pot) over a turf fire in the moorland areas of North-East Yorkshire. Turf cakes were originally unsweetened, and without fruit, a sort of griddle bread. This, however, is a sweet version popular in the late Victorian period.

**1 lb self raising flour
6 oz butter
2 oz lard
2 oz castor sugar
2 eggs
4 oz currants
milk
salt**

Makes about 9

Rub the butter into the flour. Add the sugar and currants. Beat the eggs well with a little milk and mix them in to create a soft dough. Roll out to ½ inch thick, cut into 3 inch rounds. Bake at 400°F/gas mark 6 on a greased tray for about 12 minutes, until golden brown.

Parkin

Parkin, a north country speciality, has long been associated with the 5 November bonfires and celebrations.

8 oz oatmeal
8 oz flour
1 lb treacle
8 oz butter
½ oz ground ginger
1 teaspoon sugar
¼ pint milk
1 teaspoon bicarbonate of soda

Place the oatmeal and flour in a mixing bowl and rub into it the butter. Add the ginger and sugar. Warm the treacle until it is runny, and mix in. Warm the milk, dissolve the bicarbonate of soda in it, and add to the mixture, mixing the whole to a smooth dough.

Grease a large, flat tin, and line it with greaseproof paper. Pour in the dough, spread to an even depth. Bake at 375°F/gas mark 5 for 45 minutes or until dark brown.

Cut into squares to serve.

Gingerbread

Gingerbread and ginger biscuits were associated with fairs and holidays. In some parts of the country gingerbread became known as fairings, because it could be bought from the stalls. There are several variations. Some early recipes treat gingerbread as a boiled bread pudding, which could be pressed into moulds after cooking. Another type, popular in the North, was baked as a crisp, moulded biscuit, and covered in gold foil for sale. The recipe given here is the rich cake-like version popular in the nineteenth century.

10 oz plain flour
4 oz butter
9 oz treacle
4 oz sugar
1 teaspoon bicarbonate of soda
pinch of salt
1 teaspoon ground ginger
1 teaspoon cinnamon
1 egg
¼ pint milk

Melt the butter, sugar and treacle together in a saucepan. In a mixing bowl, mix together the flour, soda, salt and spice. Make a well in the centre. Beat the egg thoroughly with the milk. Mix this and the treacle mixture into the flour and beat until smooth. Pour into a baking tin or 8″ cake tin lined with greaseproof paper. Bake for 40–45 minutes, at 350°F/gas mark 4.

Gingernuts

These are extremely simple biscuits, for which there are many early recipes.

4 oz flour (self-raising)
1 tablespoon sugar
1 teaspoon bicarbonate of soda
2 oz butter
2 tablespoons treacle or golden syrup
1 teaspoon ground ginger

Makes about 16 biscuits

Mix the flour, ginger, sugar and bicarbonate of soda in a bowl. Rub in the butter. Stir in the treacle to form a stiff paste. Divide the mixture into about 16 pieces. Roll each into a ball, flatten slightly and place on greased baking sheets. Leave plenty of room between each biscuit as they spread during cooking.

Bake for about 15 minutes, at 375° F/gas mark 5.

Curd Cheese Cake

In some markets in the north of England it is still possible to buy creamy white curds. Traditionally cheese curd is made by adding a half a pint of buttermilk to two pints of fresh (not pasteurised) milk, and then heating to boiling point, stirring occasionally with a wooden spoon. When the curds stick to the spoon they are ready. The liquid or 'whey' can be strained off through a sieve.

An alternative (and unauthentic) method, using pasteurised milk, is to add 4 beaten eggs to two pints of milk and bring gently to the boil, stirring occasionally. Reduce the heat, and the mixture should turn into a curd. Tip it into a sieve to drain.

For the pastry
8 oz flour
4 oz butter
salt
milk

For the filling
1 lb curds
4 oz granulated sugar
3 oz currants
1 egg, beaten
nutmeg

Makes 6 to 8 cakes

Make-up the pastry and roll out. Line a well-greased flan-tin or large plate with pastry. Alternatively, small cakes can be made in a bun tin or patty-pan.

Mix together the ingredients of the filling, and spread over the pastry. Bake for about 20 minutes at 375°F/gas mark 5 or until brown.

Pepper Cake

Like those other spicy confections, gingerbread and parkin, pepper cake was associated with celebrations. On the birth of a child, and at Christmas, a pepper cake was set atop a large cheese on a platter, and every visitor to the house was invited to partake. There is a carolling rhyme:

A little bit of pepper cake
A little bit of cheese
A cup of cold water
And a penny if you please.

12 oz flour
4 oz brown sugar
1 teaspoon baking powder
1 oz powdered cloves or ginger
12 oz treacle
4 oz butter
3 eggs, beaten

In a large mixing bowl, place the flour, baking powder and ginger. Warm the butter until it is very soft and cream it with the sugar. Heat the treacle until it runs and then add the treacle, beaten eggs, sugar and butter to the dry ingredients, mixing together well.

Turn the mixture into a medium size cake tin, greased and lined with greaseproof paper. Bake for 45 minutes at 325°F/gas mark 3.

Conversion Tables

Ounces	Grammes		Pints	Millilitres
1 oz	28 g			
2 oz	57 g		¼ pt	142 ml
3 oz	85 g		⅓ pt	189 ml
4 oz	113 g		½ pt	284 ml
5 oz	142 g		¾ pt	426 ml
6 oz	170 g		1 pt	568 ml
7 oz	198 g		2 pt	1.13 litre
8 oz	227 g		3 pt	1.7 litre
9 oz	255 g		4 pt	2.27 litre
10 oz	283 g			
11 oz	312 g			
12 oz	340 g			
13 oz	368 g			
14 oz	397 g			
15 oz	425 g			
1 lb	453 g			
2 lb	907 g			
3 lb	1.36 kg			
4 lb	1.81 kg			

Fahrenheit	Celsius	Gas Mark
225°F	110°C	¼
250°F	120°C	½
275°F	140°C	1
300°F	150°C	2
325°F	160°C	3
350°F	180°C	4
375°F	190°C	5
400°F	200°C	6
425°F	220°C	7
450°F	230°C	8
475°F	240°C	9

Inches	Centimetres
1 in	2.54 cm
2 in	5 cm
3 in	7.6 cm
4 in	10 cm
5 in	13 cm
6 in	15 cm
7 in	18 cm
8 in	20 cm
9 in	23 cm
10 in	25 cm
11 in	28 cm
12 in	30 cm

Index of Recipes

Glossary of Terms

Bakestone or backstone: a flat stone, sometimes built into a kitchen fireplace, which was heated for cooking oatcakes, etc.

Baste: to spoon hot fat or liquid over food (especially meat) during cooking. This is to keep the food moist and juicy.

Breadcrumbs (browned): made from de-crusted stale white bread, crushed with a rolling pin or put through a mincer, and then browned in a moderately hot oven.

Dredge (with flour, etc): to sprinkle a coat of flour over the food.

Griddle or girdle: traditionally a flat, usually circular, iron plate with handle from which it could be suspended over the fire for cooking pancakes, oatcakes, etc.

Parboil: to boil vegetables for a few minutes, as a preliminary to adding them to other ingredients, or to roasting.

Paste: the old word for pastry.

Pudding cloth: a muslin or mutton cloth used to contain a pudding within the boiling pot.

Stock: water in which meat, fish, vegetables, etc. have been boiled, and used as the base for soups, sauces and in other dishes.

Suet: the hard fat which surrounds the kidneys of cattle and sheep. You can purchase it from a butcher and chop it finely, or (as I have assumed in these recipes) buy it ready prepared in a packet.

Truffle cheese: the best cheese.

Notes

Notes

Notes

Notes

Notes

Notes

Notes

Notes